Dear God

How We P-R-A-Y Every Day

To Momma:
Thank you for decades of powerful prayers!
I will love you forever!
Love, Joshie

To Jeanie, Pax, and Zoe:
You are each an answered prayer!
You are for signs, wonders, and miracles!
Your prayers will move mountains!
Love, Mommy and Daddy

PASS IT ON
LIBRARY

Published by Pass It On Library
www.PassItOnLibrary.com

Follow us on Social @PassItOnLibrary

First Edition published in the USA in 2024 by Pass It On Library

ISBN: 979-8-9922183-0-5 (paperback)

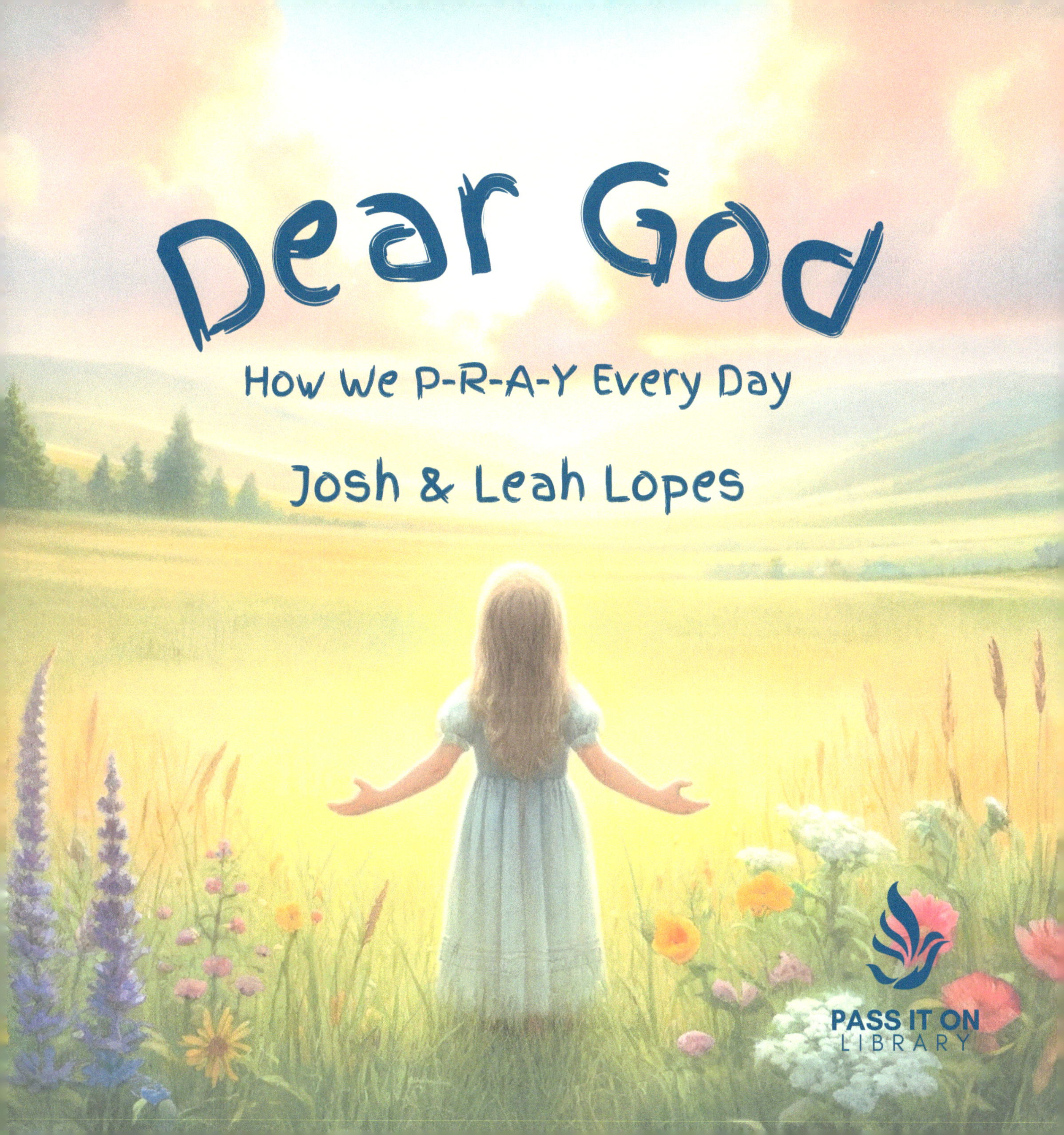

Dear God

How We P-R-A-Y Every Day

Josh & Leah Lopes

PASS IT ON
LIBRARY

Let's P-R-A-Y...it starts with "P."
PRAISE is where God lives with you and me.

Dear God, we start our prayer to You
by giving thanks for all You do.

And for who You are! We PRAISE and sing!
We clap our hands to our awesome King!

You carefully carved the valleys low.
You perfectly painted every rainbow.

You generously gave us Your only Son.
Your purpose and plans for us are already done.

We thank You for Your love, healing, and mercy.
We praise You, God, and give You all the glory.

The letter "R" reminds us to REPENT
for parts of our lives that are a little bit bent.

We are sorry, God, for the things we do that don't bring You joy or honor You.

We seek You and Your face today.
We want to turn from our sinful ways.

Please help us to do better.
Jesus, take us by the hand.
Please forgive our sin.
Please heal our land.

Despite all the things that we've done wrong,
Thank You for Your love, for still letting us belong.

The next letter in the word "PRAY"
is the letter "A"
which reminds us to "ASK,"
spelled A-S-K!

We ASK for Your blessings.
With faith, we believe
that You answer our prayers.
Your Word says we will receive.

We SEEK Your face, God,
with open hearts and open minds.
We know when we keep seeking,
Your word says that we will find.

We KNOCK on Heaven's door.
And know You'll open it for sure.
We keep on knocking because
Your grace equips us to endure.

Just like Your word reminds us,
we ask and seek and knock.
We know consistency is key
for Your Kingdom to be unlocked.

Thank You, God, for listening
when we talk to You and pray
about anything, any time,
anywhere, and any day.

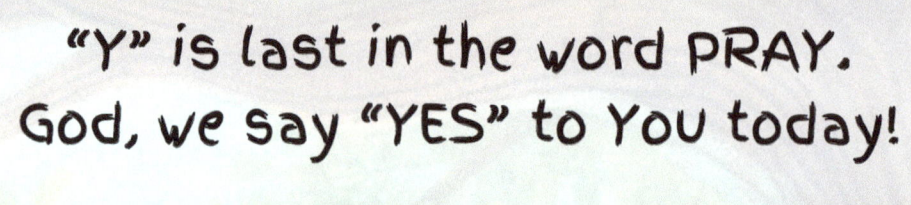

"Y" is last in the word PRAY.
God, we say "YES" to You today!

We can talk to You about people, things,
or times that make us sad.

We don't need to pretend or fake it.
Our honesty is a must.
We can tell You anything, God.
You're the one we can always trust.

About how to pray,
we don't need to make a fuss.
Because You like to hear uniquely
from each one of us.

Some of us like to sing.
Some of us like to talk.

Some of us pray by dancing,
while others take a walk.

Some of us pray by writing letters
to You about how we feel.
And others pray by listening
to Your voice and love so real.

Some of us like to pray
in the closet in our room.
Others like to pray outside
with nature in full bloom.

Whether inside or out,
whether whisper or shout,
whether together or apart,
Lord, we give You our hearts.

Thank You for sweet dreams tonight
and for a wonderful day.
Thank You, Lord, for hearing us
when we "P-R-A-Y" pray!

Amen!

Discussion Questions

What are some things you want to thank God for today?

Can you think of a time when you needed to say sorry to God or someone else? How did it feel?

What is something you'd like to ask God for right now?

How do you think God listens to our prayers?

What are some ways you like to pray—singing, talking, drawing, dancing, or something else?

PASS IT ON
LIBRARY

www.ingramcontent.com/pod-product-compliance
Lightning Source LLC
Chambersburg PA
CBHW041619120626
46551CB00003B/507